FIFTY-TWO AVOIDABLE WAYS WE WASTE MONEY THESE DAYS

BY

BISHOP OCHEI INNOCENT

Contents

DEDICATION

To the eighty-seven [87] million
Nigerians allegedly unable to spend two
dollars [$2.00] per day.

WHY THIS BOOK?

Many people cry every day that they do not have. Some go as far as blaming their stars, neighbor's and even God for their not having!

But some of us know that God even while we were yet in our mother's wombs, provided and continues to provide. God is not man that can neglect his children. The God that we worship is Jehovah Jireh: the God that provides.

The problem however is that even the little we are given, we fail to make the best use of! We spend where we should save! Little drops of water, we know forms a mighty ocean! We spend as if there is no tomorrow forgetting that Rome was not built in a day.

Unmindful, we walk around with leaking pockets. We earn but it is as if there is a physical hole in our pocket!

Rather than take stock of our actions and choices, we choose to blame the devil, witches and village people for everything. While such evil doers cannot be sincerely dismissed with a wave of the hand, truth remains that not everything can be pinned on the misdeeds of others.

We must first take a look at our own wrong choices. That is what this book is all about. While agreeing that the country can be better in all spheres, this book asks a simple question: how are you taking care of the little that God is giving you?

WARNING

This book will do you good [or better] if Jesus Christ is the foundation on which your life is built. I do not hesitate to tell you that a life without Jesus Christ is a life perpetually in crises!

Jesus Christ is the answer to all questions ever asked and will be asked by man in future. He died on the cross so that his Blood atones for the sins of man [including you and me] once and for all! Since the beginning of the earth, up to when Jesus Christ paid the price, the blood of animals and other forms of sacrifice could not permanently wash away the sins of man until Jesus Christ paid the ultimate price for me and you. Thus, he saved man from the power of sin and death for every soul that sins dies spiritually!

A soul that dies spiritually may appear to be living but is totally taken by sin and sorrow! It thrives on vices, poverty and a lack of self-control!

All you need to succeed in life are: realize the fact of Jesus Christ sacrifice and accept him as your personal Lord and Savior. Then, all other things shall be added unto you including but not limited to salvation and wisdom which we know is the answer to all challenges of life!

If you choose to go through life on your own, then, you are on your own. If you choose to depend on what failed your fore-fathers and kept your village without even something as simple as electricity for years, then, that thing will also fail you. If you choose to depend on the wisdom of man, man will fail you. Be warned that nothing in this book can work permanently for you without giving your life to Jesus Christ.

To have Jesus Christ come into your life is very simple: While this book is still in your hands, open your heart and mouth: Confess that Jesus Christ is Lord over your life and destiny. Confess that he died on the cross for your sake and that from this day on, he is in charge of your life! If you want to know that Jesus Christ is alive, pray tonight and ask for something difficult in his name, he will do it for you!

CHAPTER ONE

CAN WE START WITH SOME FOUNDATIONAL ISSUES?

1. **IGNORANCE**

   This is a very wasteful situation to be in. When you are in a state of ignorance, you will not even know that you are living a wasteful life. When you do not know this, how can you remedy the situation?

2. **LIVING A SINFUL LIFE**

   Out of the same ignorance, we call sin enjoyment. However a sinful life is a mixture of petrol and fire as far as money is concerned. Sin, to give one or two example, makes us take a girl to far places that cost money so that prying eyes will not see us. Sin makes us eat our annual salary in one night and buy even things we do not need, etc.! Living a holy life, on the other hand, opens our eyes to reality and keeps our expenses within bounds.

3. BUYING JUST TO IMPRESS OTHERS

Closely related to a life of sin are the issues of pride and ego which make us to buy luxury items, sometimes we even borrow money, just to impress our neighbors and observers. Is that not why one popular but tiny generator is called *"I better Pass My Neighbor?"*

4. BUYING JUST TO FEED YOUR EYES

A wise man buys useful things and not just beautiful things. Most of the beauty are artificial and soon fade away. That is why in Nigeria we tend to buy strong old school second-hand items popularly called _"Tokumbo"_ instead of some of the fanciful but expensive models of today that spoil or damage even before the seller finishes issuing the receipt!

5. **EATING OUT IN EXPENSIVE HANG-OUTS**
Many of us eat in places we know we cannot afford. Such ego trips add nothing to our bank account but leaves holes in our pockets.

6. **EATING OUT ALL THE TIME**
This is a twin sister to the point above. Why not cook at home since it is cheaper and more hygienic? One can eat out once in a while but not all the time.

7. **SHOPPING JUST BECAUSE OF THE LABELS!**
Some buy no matter the price just as long as they are able to boast or show off the label. "Oh, my bag is

Gucci or something." If you can afford it, no problem but if nothing, there is a problem!

Chapter Two

BANKING ISSUES

8. NOT HAVING A BANK ACCOUNT AT ALL

This means that a lot of cash that should have gone to the bank is always with you and you can always dip your hand into it and spend impulsively. Many times, after you have spent a lot, you are not able to give account because such monies have no record and may have gone into avoidable expenditure!

9. NOT AUDITING BANK CHARGES

We lose a lot of money by not asking for our bank

statement from time to time. Sometimes, either by error of omission or commission bankers over-charge and if you do nothing about it, that money is lost. Remember that little drops of water form a mighty ocean!

10.   **RUNNING A CURRENT ACCOUNT**

Small and medium savers or companies should note that monthly bank charges amount to a lot at the end of each year! Check with your bank and see. Should you not rather operate a savings account and make electronic transfers instead of checks?

11.   **TAKING BANK LOANS WE DO NOT NEED**

I know a pastor that took a bank loan from a community bank at cut throat interest rate, to build a non-commercial church auditorium! Banks give loans for business and a church is not a commercial venture. Loans are also time bound and may attract compound interests.

12.   **MAKING LARGE CASH DEPOSITS**

This now attracts bank fines when over five hundred thousand naira in Nigeria. Other countries have similar policy. So why allow your cash to stockpile?

13.   **VISITING BANKS ALL THE TIME**

Most rich men do not visit banks. They make inter-bank transfers and budget their periodic expenses so that they do not have to visit banks too often. Each trip cost money and you waste

time in bank queues. You
know too that time is money.

14. **BANKING WITH A
BANK WITHOUT A BRANCH
NEAR YOU**

This can be avoided. Check
the high cost of travelling to
and fro. Then pick a local
bank near you.

15. **SHUNNING
ELECTRONIC BANKING**

We are now in a cashless
era. Electronic banking
means that you handle less
cash and leave nothing at
home for thieves and rats to
take away.

Chapter Three
COMMUNICATION ISSUES

16.   GOING OUT WHEN YOU CAN TALK ON PHONE

Many people are yet to recover from the gone analogue days when we need to leave home in order to see our relations, attend meetings or do business. Thus, we waste money travelling for simple things we can talk over on the phone. Even village people have telephones now.

Town unions and clubs now do video conferencing! We can life stream meetings or Skype them!

There is also an added advantage of talking on the phone: telephones keep record of all discussions! So some transactions and agreements cannot be denied! And if it is a meeting, money which would have been spent typing minutes is saved amongst others!

17. PHONING WHEN YOU CAN TEXT

Every form of communication is meant to be short, simple, straight to the point and specific. Phoning is charged on duration per second. Therefore, the shorter the duration the better! So, why not text, instead of calling? **"MacLean's Magazine"** of Canada is credited with the advice that: *"the easiest way to become bankrupt is to own a mobile phone"*!

18. BUYING DATA FROM RETAILERS

Why not buy data in bulk and from the network owners? The more you buy the cheaper it is?

19.   NOT BUYING DATA FROM DISCOUNT COMPANIES

There are companies that give discount when you buy data from them. Examples in Africa are Recharge-and-Get-Paid, Quick-teller, etc.

20.   BURNING DATA JUST TO POST SELFIES ONLINE!

This one needs no further explanation. Some, including fathers and husbands take from three to a dozen pictures of their ugly faces to post daily on social media. Making you wonder whether they are entering a beauty pageant!

21.   CHATTERING ON PHONE

Telephone is a business tool. It is not meant for social chats per se. define what you want to say and say it quickly. Do not dilly- dally on the phone. If you do, your money is going.

Chapter Four

ENERGY ISSUES

22.   **USING GENERATOR INSTEAD OF SOLAR**
This leads to colossal waste of money. Solar taps power from the sun and takes minimum maintenance. We now have solar lamps, fans, stoves, etc. Almost everything! It takes away the high cost of electricity and petrol on generators!

23.   **DRIVING WHEN ALONE IN THE CAR**
You are wasting a lot of gas. Why not take a public transport which is by far cheaper? Must you massage your ego with a car?

24. DRIVING TO SHOW OFF

This is similar to point [22] above. Imagine all the gas you could have saved by swallowing your pride? Some folks are known to buy new cars at Christmas time for instance only to sell it at give-away price after the festive period. Is that not folly?

25. LEAVING ELECTRICITY ON WHEN NOT NEEDED

Go and get pre-paid meter. Under estimated billing I was paying over ten thousand naira per month. Now with prepared, I spend less than three thousand! Once you install pre-paid meter, ensure that you put off all the things you do not need.

Chapter Five

ECONOMIC ISSUES

26.   BUYING THINGS WITHOUT COMMERCIAL VALUE

This has to do mainly with domestic appliances such as washing machines, deep freezers; multiple cars, etc. commercialize the ones you can.

27.   PAYING RENT INSTEAD OF OWNING THE HOUSE

I know people who choose to pay rent in high profile areas instead of own homes of their own in other less popular places. Whatever their reason, a tenant is still a tenant and that area you over-look now will soon be a city!

28. NOT HELPING YOUR CHILDREN WITH THEIR HOME WORK

This is penny wise pound foolish because if the child fails, you will pay another year school fees! So why not help the poor child or employ a home teacher for him or her? In the long run, it is cheaper.

29. BEING ON SOCIAL MEDIA ALL THE TIME

You are wasting time, burning data and doing nothing in particular. Social media must have a purpose and time or you waste your money.

30. NOT USING APPS

Most apps run free while most websites charge money to allow you down load anything.

31.   NOT TAKING ADVANTAGE OF PROMOS

Watch out for promos in all spheres of life. Companies and organizations do all kinds of promos. Watch out and take advantage, to save money.

32.   EXPENSIVE WEDDINGS

Avoid them. Even if you drop a billion, the people will finish it and some will still get neither food nor drink. It has been like that and will continue because of cheats and thieves!

33.   EXPENSIVE BURIALS

This same thing as [33] above goes for burials. Some will never be satisfied no

matter what you do.
Remember that life
continues after the burial.

34. PUTTING DEAD ONES IN MORTUARY FOR AGES

What do you want to do that
has never been done before?
In the end, the corpse will
still decay. Stop wasting your
money. If the money is
available why not set up a
foundation to help the needy
in the name of the dead?
That will make better social
sense!

35. EXPENSIVE HANDSETS THAT YOU ONLY USE TEN PERCENT OF THE CAPACITY

Why buy phones that
attract thieves, especially when
you do   not even use the
sophisticated phone to capacity?

36. NOT HAVING A GARDEN

Produce your own food if you can. Do not buy everything.

37. **NOT EXERCISING**
This leads to obesity and ill-health and this can take one to hospital where huge bills are often paid.

38. **LACK OF MAINTENANCE**
When you fail to maintain some machines and generators, you end up spending to replace them. Changing car oil after some mileage is financial wisdom!

39. **GREEDINESS**
This makes you buy and grab what you cannot eat or use for life. Resist the urge and it will flee from you.

40. **SENDING CHILDREN TO LONG DISTANCE SCHOOLS**

This makes you enroll for school bus or some form of transportation. Both of them take extra money. Look for schools near your house and enroll your children. Do not be emotionally involved with some schools just because they have reputation. When have that kind of money, send your children where ever you want but not when you are managing!

41.   **NOT TRADING ONLINE**
Wake up please. Everything you need on earth is just a phone call away! Learn to buy and sell online. It saves cost and time of going to market. It saves the cost of renting shops and sometimes the goods are cheaper because the seller is selling in large quantity.

42. TAKING UNWANTED TITLES

They put you in tight corners and make you live above your means! It gives you a big name that kills the dog and drills holes in your financial pocket.

43. AVOIDABLE COURT CASES

Lawyers cost money and so do postponement of cases! You have to pay transport each time you go to court and in the end, if found guilty, you might be asked to pay a fine or damages!

44. UNWANTED VISITORS

Not only did you not invite them, you did not plan for them. They eat your food, waste your time and even later gossip about you. While you may not be able to do away with them completely,

find ways to minimize their
number and frequency!

Chapter Six

TRAVELLING THINGS

45. NOT BUYING AIRTICKET FROM ONE SOURCE

When travelling, buy your tickets from one source. That way, you will attract good discounts and recognition! You are throwing away money by buying from different places.

46. NOT BUYING IN GROUP

If travelling in a group, negotiate for discounts. Most airlines and motor companies give handsome discounts for group purchases.

47.   WHEN BOOKING FOR HOTEL ACCOMMODATION

Negotiate for group discounts as well as discounts for long stay. I once got a room free for every seven days booked! Ask and you shall receive!

48.   FIND OUT WHAT IS CHEAPER IN YOUR COUNTRY

Buy and take it along with you. I once found that something I bought for a dollar in my country sold for seven dollars in a neighboring country!

49.   TAKE BEVERAGES ALONG FOR BREAKFAST

Some breakfast cost your limbs when not at home. With beverages, you can boil water and take tea in the

morning with some not to
expensive biscuits.

**50.   BOOK HOTELS WITH
BED AND BREAKFAST IF
YOU CAN**

That in theory saves you the
cost of breakfast! It should
be said that most times, the
cost of the breakfast is
worked into what you pay
but you never really can say!
It might be a big saving.

**51.   NEVER CHOOSE A
HOTEL IN HASTE**

Do a thorough research on
hotels in the city you are
going. You will be shocked to
find cheaper and better
equipped but not advertised
facilities!

**52.   FIND OUT ALL THE
PERKS**

Some hotels have free Wi-Fi
facilities and other perks.
Grab them. They save you a

lot of money, especially in calling home.
By the way, remember to roam your phone or use the local line in your host country!

The End

OTHER BOOKS BY BISHOP OCHEI

1. Something Worse Than Witchcraft And Acidic Prayers To Destroy It.
2. Productivity: How to Increase Your Income a Thousand fold!
3. How to Sell the Seemingly Unsellable.
4. Six Things You Must Do Before Age Sixty.
5. Ten Things I like About Africa's Richest Man.
6. How To Increase Your Ministerial Connections
7. The Best Thing You Can Do For Yourself As A Christian

ABOUT THE AUTHOR

Bishop Innocent Ochei is a Research Enthusiast and President of New Dimension Seminaries International.

He is married to Elizabeth, a Pentecostal prophetess and they are blessed with four God-fearing children.

THANK YOU FOR READING

Please if you have any suggestions for the next edition or any other comment feel free to contact the author on:

newochei@gmail.com

You can also reach him for counseling and prayers on the same address.